How to Make Cash Today with Scrap Metal Recycling

Miles H. Broderson
www.milesbroderson.com

ABUNDANT HARVEST
PUBLISHING

Editing/Formatting: Erik V. Sahakian
Cover Design/Layout: Andrew Enos

Library of Congress Control Number: 2022902926

ISBN 978-1-7377261-9-7
First Printing: February 2022

FOR INFORMATION CONTACT:

Abundant Harvest Publishing
www.abundantharvestpublishing.com

Printed in the United States of America

This book is dedicated to my beautiful wife, Julie, who has stood by my side and supported me through all of my ups and downs as an entrepreneur. Without the presence of her and her two children, Taylor and Lindy, in my life, I am certain that this book would have never existed. This book is also dedicated to my parents and every one of my friends and relatives, both close and distant. This book is dedicated to all of the people who have helped me through hard times and helped me celebrate good times as well!

Contents

Part Three

A Word from the Author

When I was 17 years old I discovered what entrepreneurship was for the very first time. At the time I had never heard that word before and had no idea what it meant. I was over at my friend's house doing what 17-year-olds do on a Friday evening, if you get my drift. My friend was in college and we were talking about the future and what we wanted to become one day.

I had been explaining to him that I couldn't understand what my position was in the world, but I knew how to turn profits and I wanted to work for myself. I was still working at my first job installing garage doors and delivering firewood every other day after work and on weekends. That same year I had also taken over my grandfather's Christmas tree lot in our small town, selling Christmas trees between Thanksgiving and Christmas after he had passed away.

As I was explaining to him all of the things I was up to and my plans for the future, he cleared his throat as if he wanted to interrupt me midsentence, which he did. He interrupted with four words that I would never forget. He said, "Dude, you're an entrepreneur." At that moment in time I was ill read and uninformed as to what that word even meant. However, from that day forward

I began my journey and search for the truth stated within those four words.

It didn't happen immediately, but over the course of the following five years, I began studying the subject of entrepreneurship, devouring books, listening to CDs, and watching whatever was available to help me better understand the subject. I began placing myself in uncomfortable situations, some of which downright scared me due to my lack of knowledge on how to do what I was trying to do. Some worked out in my favor and some did not.

I began doing all of this in search of answers to most of our biggest questions in life as entrepreneurs. Those questions being: what is my purpose and where is my place as an entrepreneur? Through a process of trial and error, and over the course of a decade or so, the answers to both of those questions began to reveal itself with each new endeavor.

In this book, I hope to give those of you who are new to entrepreneurship a single stepping stone and a platform to stand on so that you can see possibilities that you couldn't see before reading this book. Although your journey as an entrepreneur will likely resemble a Bollinger band on a stock chart, always try to remember this quote by J.P. Morgan: "Go as far as you can see, when you get there you'll be able to see farther."

This book was simply designed to help you expand your horizons to see new income earning possibilities. It is my intent to help put more income earning tools in your tool belt as you embark upon your entrepreneurial endeavors. I sincerely hope to help improve your life financially and as a new entrepreneur through many of the examples illustrated in this book.

Enjoy!

Part One

[14]

Introduction

Congratulations on the choice you have made to increase your income and step into the world of entrepreneurship. Scrap metal recycling is a great avenue to do exactly that. One of the main reasons for this is because it has become overlooked by so many. Especially those of you who are millennials.

Most people who are looking for ways to earn income fast are out there looking for a get-rich-quick strategy. They just want to open a computer and "set it and forget it." I don't know about you, but I have met very few people who have actually pulled this off long term. While there are a number of online strategies that do work for some, they aren't easy, and they require effort just like anything else.

The good news is there's a much less complicated strategy, like this one. Remember that whether you're online or offline, the recipe for increased income isn't microwavable. It often takes some slow and steady baking to make that bread rise. Our goal here is simply to get you to start making some money quickly. Once you prove that it's possible to yourself, then the rest is up to you.

This book will show you how to run the race and even

hand you the baton, but this is *your* race and you've gotta run it.

In later lessons you will learn all you need to know to start making money quickly. For now, I'm going to make two claims about reading this book: first, you'll be exposed to an industry that you may not be aware of or understand currently, and second, you'll learn how to quickly make a good portion of your money back from the purchase of this book. You will probably even turn a handsome profit above and beyond your investment in this book, if you follow the steps, if you "take action" and follow through. So without further ado, let's get right into it!

Lesson 1

Developing an "Eye" for Scrap Metal Profits

Make cash today! This may be the only step you need to see the bigger picture and it is my hope that this is true for you. Before you learn all that there is to know about recycling metals, let's get you some cash rolling in as fast as possible.

Let's do an exercise right now to open your eyes to what is possible. This is the part where you get your money back from the purchase of this book, if you follow instructions and execute. I want you to look around your home for a minute. If you are not at home, I want you to imagine that you are. Notice the kitchen stove, the microwave, the refrigerator, if you open your kitchen drawer you will likely have some silverware. Now notice any wall fixtures and metal lamps plugged into the walls, even the television. These are all worth money! Please don't get me wrong, I realize that you're probably not going to scrap any of your personal furniture or fixtures. Later in this book I will show you how to get them in large quantities and turn them into cash!

What I want to encourage you to do now is scan your entire house inside and out, top to bottom, and front to back for any and all unwanted metal items. You're going to be gathering a pile together and you're going to want it to be as heavy as you can possibly make it.

Next, let's take a look at the back patio. Most homes or apartments will have some type of patio furniture out back— there's even a good chance of seeing an old barbecue as well. These are also worth money at the scrapyard. Let's check the side yard of your home for metal of any kind. We're going to be looking for old lawnmowers, old bicycles, old weights, broken swing sets, metal storage racks, etc. ANYTHING METAL!

Now to the garage. If you do not have a garage, I would be willing to bet that you know somebody who does. I'd recommend that you let your neighbors know what you're doing as well in order to see if they have any unwanted metal items in their garages, or on their properties they'd like to offload as well before you head off for your test run.

You can usually uncover some long forgotten gems in the garage. We want to look for old car parts, especially car batteries, transmissions, alternators, starters, etc. You get the point. Next, look for any old metal tools such as wrenches, hammers, even old extension cords...anything predominantly made of metal. Try to find old weight sets, plates, barbells, dumbbells, kettlebells, etc. Again, anything metal! Continue on like this until you've searched every room in the house including the attic and basement, if you have them.

Lesson 2

Preparing for the Test Run

Now that you've identified a number of metal items all throughout your home, I want you to understand that all of these things are worth money and have scrap value. Also understand that almost every household on every street likely has as much as you do, if not potentially much more! This is good news for you! At this point, I want you to decide how many of these items have reached the end of their shelf life and are no longer needed around the house.

Now a disclaimer and a warning. If you are young or old, and you happen to be living with your parents, do not take Mom's pots or pans to the scrapyard for cash. If you do…she might give us both a frying pan upside the head for that one! Just get her permission first. Leave Dad's tools alone too, until you get the okay from him.

Moving on. Gather up any metal items you no longer need as they are just sitting there earning you nothing. This is where the fun begins! You are about to do your first test run! This will be your first time making money from scrap metal recycling. The purpose for the test run is for you to get an immediate return on investment (ROI) in this book. I want you to have this experience before you finish this book, so that you actually realize this is well within your reach and it is tangible. You'll walk away with some cash, or a check in your name, as soon as you execute on the following action steps laid out for you.

Lesson 3

Locating a Scrapyard

Your next step is going to be making some phone calls to the scrapyards in your local area. It is likely that your area has more than one; if so, this is good news for your wallet! Eventually you will be calling every scrapyard in your area looking for the highest price per ton. However, for the purpose of your test run, use the one closest to your home. You'll want to get on your computer or smart phone and key in the words "scrap metal recycling company" with the name of your town or city included.

Give them a call and make sure they're open for business. You will also want to ask them about their business hours and what time they except their last customer of the day, knowing this will save you time. For example, scrapyards often stay open till 4:30 or 5 p.m., but they require everybody to be there 15 minutes before the time they close so that they're not staying open for a line of people after they close. They will often turn you away if you get there one minute before they close, and they should.

Lesson 4

Things to Remember on the Test Run

Now that you've identified a scrapyard close to home, and you've figured out their business hours, it's time to go get your money!

You will need transportation of some sort obviously. If you don't have a pickup truck, or even a car with a trunk, then you will need to talk to a parent, relative, friend, or neighbor. Assuming you have, or will find transportation of some sort, the next thing you will want to make sure you have is a valid photo identification card, or a valid driver's license. They will require this at the scrapyard. They will most likely be taking your thumbprint as well, prior to you receiving your money. At most scrapyards, they do this with all new customers. This may change from county to county, state to state, or country to country depending upon where you're located on the globe.

Lesson 5

What to Expect

When you arrive at the scrapyard, you will likely see an entrance sign, and potentially a line of cars. If so, get your spot in line because it will be worth the wait. It will help you understand the process, even if you don't have much metal with you. In the next section of this book, you'll learn how to dramatically increase the amount of metal you acquire and money you make. Remember this is just your test run.

When you arrive at the front of the line, if there is one, you will be greeted by an employee. He or she will instruct you where to park and how to separate your metals. In the next section of this book we will break down all the different metals for you, so that you can understand how to make more money with some of the same exact items. For now, let's just focus on you getting a return on the investment of your purchase of this book.

Lesson 6

Turning Your First Profit

When you get to the scale they will likely ask you for identification. There will probably be two different scales: one for your ferrous metals and one for your nonferrous metals. They will direct you as to which material goes to which scale. They will also likely have sorting bins for you to separate your materials. Just follow their instructions. After you give them your identification, they will make a copy and keep it on file. Give them your thumbprint as well.

After they have weighed your material across their scale, they will likely tell you what your total is. You want to make sure that they've accurately weighed and paid you before you sign your receipt. They will give you a receipt either right there at the scale or at a separate window, when they're handing you your cash or check. Just make sure all the line items on your receipt match all the materials you brought in. Also, pay attention to the scale while they're weighing your scrap. Sometimes they will "forget" to weigh an item or two of yours, and that's just money out of your pocket!

At this point you will have completed your test run. Depending on the scrap market price at the time you have completed this first section of the book, I am certain you realize my claim is true. I'm confident that you now know how to make money in a way that you may not have been aware of before. I am also confident that you have recovered the majority of the money you spent on this easy-to-read, eye-opening, first section of this book. It is my hope that you have even turned a profit above and beyond what you have spent on this purchase. In either case, give yourself a round of applause. You have now learned how to turn your first profit with scrap metal recycling!

Lesson 7

How to Increase Your Scrap Metal Volume and Profit

I'm going to ask you to ponder something. Do you want to stop making money right here? Or do you want to learn how to make 10x, 20x, even 100x the amount of money that you just earned with this one simple test run. You have only seen the tip of the iceberg! You haven't yet even scratched the surface of what is possible with scrap metal recycling. It is more than possible to earn between $1,000 to $3,000 or more in your first month of focused hustle.

In the next section of this book we dive deeper into many of the possible avenues for you, as well as how to do them. You will learn how to make your phone ring for cheap, and for free. You will learn how to answer the phone, as well as the right questions to ask to maximize your income. You will learn advanced marketing tactics, both online and offline.

Part 2 of this volume is designed to expand your horizons and increase your ability to acquire larger quantities of scrap metal. This of course means that you will also understand how to acquire larger quantities of cash in your pocket as the two go hand in hand.

Please understand something. Education is expensive no matter how you get it. You can take the long way of hard knocks, losses, and trial and error, or you can learn from someone who has been down that road once before. In fact, in this case thousands of times before! I once heard that having a conversation with a wise man can save somebody 10 years of trial and error. In my journey, I have found that to be 100% true.

In the next section, I will make the claim that you're going to make your money back on your investment and a huge percentage more. However, the caveat to make it happen is…YOU MUST apply yourself and take action the same way you did with the test run. You will need to step up your hustle a bit. This book is designed to take you as far as you want to go with scrap metal recycling. Part 2 is a very easy read. It was designed to keep "you" the reader interested. It is filled with stories of people and their experiences on their journey to success with scrap metal recycling.

Each person in Part 2 has developed their own strategy for becoming successful in this industry. If one were to model themselves and their efforts after the people in Part 2, they would likely obtain similar results. These strategies are for those of you who would like to obtain volumes of scrap metal on a commercial level. All the examples in the next section of the book will give you insight as to how to make a full-time income with scrap metal recycling.

Sharing insight to this "overlooked" industry has been my pleasure! This is because of the fact that this may have empowered you to change your life for the better. My efforts in creating this content have been sincere and with the best of intentions. I truly hope this has served you, and will bring positive results to you for many years to come. See you in Part 2...

Part Two

Introduction

Congratulations on your decision to move forward with your personal development and your training. You've gotten to this point because you decided you want to step up your game. I commend you for making the decision to expand your horizons. As promised in the previous section, we will delve deeper into the fundamentals.

Here I will give you some strategies to earn even more money with scrap metal recycling. Here you will learn beginner strategies that will be informative and they will teach you how to get the most out of your scrap metal collections. Here we will get straight to the point. This will teach you the basics of what you need to know to generate more cash in your pocket as fast as you apply the knowledge.

Before you get started, it is important to know that this is going to be a fast track, straight to the point, no nonsense type of training. Each topic could literally occupy 40 hours of your time or more if I were going to give you everything there is to know about all of these topics. For your convenience and to make the best use of your time, I have decided to condense this down to make it easy to digest and apply in the real world.

The basics I'm going to teach you in this section of the book will involve off-line marketing and online marketing. You will learn how to answer the phone correctly, and some of the right questions to ask when you answer the phone. This will give you insight so that you're not going into calls blindly and having to struggle for words in front of your customers. When they call, you will already be well-versed in what to say and how to respond, both with text messaging and on phone calls.

If you apply the knowledge you learn here, I am confident that you will make your money back and then some, simply by not making rookie mistakes. You will have the ability to increase profits with a true understanding of the material you're dealing with. If you can learn to think long-term, meaning week by week and month by month, instead of day by day, you will quickly see the knowledge you gain here will help you earn hundreds, if not thousands of dollars. It can also save you hundreds, if not thousands of dollars, in costly mistakes.

Understanding the cleaning process will make you a lot more money over time. In fact, all of the steps in this process will collectively work toward allowing you to make large percentages of return on your investment within a short period of time, if you apply yourself and take action. With this introduction being out of the way now, let's get right into it!

Lesson 8

How to Identify Different Types of Metal

This subject is important for you to understand because little, common mistakes can add up over time. Understanding this subject first will help you retain as much profit as possible. Here is where we will make sure that we patch up any cracks or holes you may have in your money-making boat to success before you ever set it in the water. Your competitors will be missing some of these bits of information—this will allow you to advance on them rapidly!

Example:

Let's say that your knowledge of this information helps you save and earn only an extra $20 per day (assuming that you're taking weekends off—not recommended). That's when some of your competitors will be sleeping and out playing with their friends. Your competitors don't take the extra steps instructed in this program and they will be losing that same $20 per day.

They are costing themselves an additional $400 per

month minimum! This is an extra $400 per month that you are gaining. This could be an insurance payment, a cell phone payment, or (depending on how much you eat) groceries for nearly a month. At the end of the year, this kind of money could send you on a vacation. If you decide to save it, it could pay for Christmas presents. This could be that down payment on a car or truck you've been needing. You get the point.

I would recommend that you apply this savings toward your advertising, if possible. For now, let's get you to understand metals.

You will be dealing with two types of metal. These are known as ferrous metals and nonferrous metals. Your bread and butter is going to be the ferrous metals. You will get more of these types of metals than you will nonferrous metals. Think of these ferrous metals as the cake. The nonferrous metals will be the frosting and the cherry on top as well.

The ferrous metals you collect are generally sold as:

Prepared iron: # 1 iron (most profitable).

Unprepared iron: # 2 iron (second most profitable).

Tin metal and appliances (third most profitable).

Below are the common types of ferrous metals that you will be seeing the most of on a regular basis:

Appliances: washers, dryers, refrigerators, stoves, microwaves, deep freezers, water heaters, furnaces, air conditioning units, etc.

Bicycles: mountain bikes, street bikes, dirt bikes, and children's bikes.

Car parts: bumpers, brake pads, rotors, axles, fenders, leaf springs, shocks, coils, steel wheels, metal rims, and more.

Gym equipment: barbell weights, dumbbell weights, barbell bars, stationary equipment, treadmills, elliptical machines, and more.

Household items: pots and pans, tables, chairs, patio furniture, lamps, candleholders, and wall decorations.

Tin metal: tin siding, sheet metal, tin cans, and tin fencing (the category of tin metal is so broad that nearly all the metals listed here will fall under it at the scrapyard).

It is important to understand that tin will usually be the lowest priced metal that you can sell at the scrapyard. This is why we are introducing you to a "cleaning process" in the next lesson. This makes metals that fall under the tin category more profitable, if done correctly.

Okay, at this point you have learned about the

majority of ferrous metals that you will be dealing with, collecting, and making money from.

The nonferrous metals you collect are listed below:

Aluminum: old sheet aluminum, cast aluminum, extruded aluminum, aluminum rims, etc.

Brass: yellow and red.

Copper: bright and shiny copper wire stripped, # 1 copper tubing, # 2 copper tubing, etc.

Electric motors: electric motors are generally extracted from other items (more about these later).

Insulated copper wire: more about this in the next lesson; typically, the result of extracting.

Lead: car batteries, fishing weights, wheel weights, etc.

Stainless steel: freezers, handrails, forks and knives, barbecues, water valves, etc.

Radiators: copper, brass, aluminum (more about the cleaning process later).

Listed above are eight categories of nonferrous metals you will be dealing with on a regular basis. These are all usually much more profitable than your ferrous metals.

In our cleaning process lesson of this book, you will learn how to extract these nonferrous metals from certain items to increase the value before going to the scrapyard to maximize your profit.

Listed below are some sources and examples of the type of items that are considered nonferrous metals:

Aluminum: cookware, pots and pans, car rims, truck rims, window frames, patio furniture, aluminum boats, aluminum siding, aluminum wire, aluminum antennas, aluminum satellite dishes.

Brass: faucets, sprinkler heads, bullet shells, water valves, water spigots, etc.

Copper: copper tubing, insulated copper wire, stripped copper wire, aluminum copper radiators, etc.

Listed below are some extractable ferrous metals you will commonly collect in your travels, on your journey with making money in scrap metal recycling. Keep in mind there are many other extractable objects in addition to the ones you will be seeing here. These are just going to be the most common ones that you will find.

You'll be surprised at how many different items have extractable nonferrous metal in them as you progress within this industry and start to gain experience over time. For now, let's just focus on the fundamentals to give you a basic understanding that will be enough to get you going and making money fast.

Your list of the most common scrap metal items to expect in your travels are as follows: appliances, dishwashers, microwaves, ceiling fans, any fan, washers and dryers, barbecues, recreational vehicles, bicycles, motorcycles, lawnmowers, crutches, kitchen sinks, bathtubs, and more.

Lesson 9

How to "Clean" Material (Learn to Make the Most Profit on Each Item Whenever Possible)

So it's true that a dollar saved is a dollar earned. This is where you're going to master the art of saving as well as earning on your journey to success. In the previous lesson is a list of items you will frequently come across in your travels with scrap metal recycling. These items will all typically have extractable nonferrous metal attached to them. This means more profit for you!

The cleaning process mentioned previously is a procedure by which you will extract nonferrous metals from ferrous metals. For example, if you happen to run across a washer or a dryer, you can take the back cover off the washing machine or dryer, and remove the electric motor and all the electrical wires from that washer or dryer. Once you've extracted this material, the copper wiring and the electric motor (although they are not very much weight) can be sold at a higher value than if they were left in the washer or dryer without being extracted. Every little bit adds up.

Doing what it takes to extract something that is only valued at $4.00 can really add up over the course of 100 extractions in a month or so. Especially since it only takes you a couple minutes each time.

When you come across a cast iron or stainless steel sink with the faucet still attached, you will want to remove the faucet because it is typically made of brass, which is worth more than stainless steel and cast iron when it is in its raw form. Raw form meaning no other type of metal is attached to it. Once you do this to the sink the value of the sink itself actually goes up as well because now you have clean cast iron or stainless steel. However, even though the brass is worth more than both stainless steel and cast iron, if you leave it attached and sell it as is, you will be given a lower price for everything because it is considered "dirty" and the scrapyard will have to do the work of separating the metals. Often they will try to purchase this at the lowest possible rate, which will cost you money. If you had just taken the time to remove the faucet, your profit on both materials could quadruple or better. The same is true of all materials listed previously that are subject to extracting nonferrous metal.

The cleaning process is a fairly simple process that will require a few tools of the trade.

Note: If you are not interested in learning about the tools of the trade because you already have them, you can skip this next lesson and go right to the story of Jeff's free Craigslist marketing strategy.

Lesson 10

A Few Tools You Will Want to Acquire

Below are a few tools of the trade. Only one of them is really necessary aside from reliable transportation. But to maximize profits, I would recommend you work toward getting some of these tools, preferably all of them. Some are cheap, some are not. However, having them will speed up the process and streamline the work of cleaning the material to extract more profit from it.

It's important to note that cleaning the material does increase profit; however, it is not necessary. You can take the material in and sell it, as what we call "dirty," for a lower price. All this means is that the material is not 100% of the commodity it is being sold as. In other words, it is considered contaminated due to attachments such as other types of metals, rubber, plastic, things of this nature.

So if you can't get your hands on these tools listed below, do not get discouraged. Just be working toward it and don't let lack of funds stop you. All you truly need is reliable transportation and the will to make this happen.

When you have a little money set aside and I'm talking about less than $100, I would recommend you visit a flea market on the weekends. At a flea market you never know for sure what you're buying, so thoroughly test out anything before you buy it and make sure it works. This will generally get you by for a while until you can afford more quality tools.

The list of tools is as follows:

Transportation: preferably a truck. Again, if you don't have one yet, do not let that discourage you. I've seen this done out of the trunk of countless cars and minivans. I've even seen people attach bicycles to makeshift wagons so they could haul more scrap. With this set up, I have seen people actually walk out of a scrapyard with $40 in their hands.

Dolly: preferably with smaller hard wheels, not air. Air tires tend to go flat at the worst possible times. Smaller wheels make loading things such as refrigerators and other bulky items much easier to tilt.

Tin snips: preferably heavy duty.

Hand grinder: my experience is that most of these last for quite a while. At first, don't worry about the brand; just try to get your hands on one ($30-$50 is a fair price for a used one with a decent brand name). You want to buy metal cutting blades for these (less than $20 total cost on the blades). This will be one of the expensive tools, but you'll make your money back on the investment quickly, if you're hustling.

Chop saw: note, this is optional. A used one should run you $75-$120. It comes in very handy to have a chop saw somewhere in your workstation for the cleaning process. Most tasks that you will use a chop saw for can also be done with the grinder, especially at a beginner's level. If you don't have a lot of money right now, you can leave this out. It's not absolutely necessary. If that's the case, then just stick with the grinder.

Gloves: thick leather gloves. When you're grinding, and I mean literally grinding with your hand grinder, you will be shooting metal flakes and these flakes can be hot enough to burn your skin. Any type of cloth glove will help, but leather provides a much stronger and more protective barrier. Get leather if you can.

Safety glasses/sunglasses: use common sense. Protect your eyes. Your safety is in your hands and it is up to you to protect.

Again, the most important tool of the trade is having transportation and a willingness to make things happen. On a side note, you will actually acquire some of the tools of the trade on the jobs you perform. People tend to get rid of these sort of things for various reasons. You'll see once you've been doing this for a while.

At this point, you have been informed about some of the most common types of metals that you will be profiting from. You have also been informed about some of the tools of the trade. In the next lesson, we are going to jump right into how to get your phone ringing for free, as well as how to do it cheaply. This will assist you in obtaining the material in your possession as fast as possible.

It's important that we skip ahead to the part where you start collecting the material because you will need to have it before you can clean it. So let's talk about what is necessary to get that phone ringing!

Lesson 11

How to Dominate Both Online and Offline Advertising

This lesson is going to be a little bit longer (spread out over several lessons) because it's going to have multiple options for you depending upon your ability to spend money or not. We are going to start with the way to do this for free for those of you that don't necessarily have the financial ability to pay for the cheap advertising that you will learn about next. For those of you that do have the money for cheap ads, I highly recommend that you do both once you learn about the strategies. Both strategies are very effective. If you implement them both, your results will increase by a considerable amount.

In the following lessons you will learn about some key strategies for both offline and online advertising. These strategies will be both free and inexpensive to get you started making money and building your clientele base with very little out-of-pocket expense. Due to the following lesson being a bit longer of a read, the following section is laid out in the form of a story for entertainment value. However, the stories are in fact based on actual events that took place. The names have been changed to protect identities and for liability purposes. After reading these examples, you will come to understand why. These examples are worth paying close attention to because they illustrate the difference between what some are willing to do to succeed and what some would never do.

You are about to read about a scrapper named Jeff and his determination to succeed using free marketing tactics through the online platform most of us know all too well, Craigslist.

Lesson 12

Jeff's Strategy for Making Profits from Craigslist for Free

In this lesson you will learn about Jeff's unconventional, yet highly effective free marketing strategy using Craigslist. Let's call this Craigslist Method #1, the first free method of making money on Craigslist without spending any money on advertising.

In this lesson we're going to use Jeff as an example. Jeff was a hustler; he had ambition and a dream of being able to make money with no job and no boss. From the time he was young, he wanted nothing more than to work for himself.

One day, Jeff decided that he was not going to live another day without taking action toward achieving his dream of controlling his own destiny.

Jeff had weekends off at his construction job where he put in 40 hours plus per week. One Saturday morning, he decided to take action instead of his usual weekend routine with the boys. Jeff got on the internet and went to Craigslist.

On the homepage, Jeff noticed a list of categories such as: for sale, services, business, and many others. Jeff clicked on the "for sale" section of Craigslist and he scrolled down until he saw the word "free." It was listed as a subcategory under the "for sale" section.

He went ahead and clicked on "free." When he did this he noticed a whole list of items that were posted for free. He noticed that a lot of them were made of metal, such as bicycles, car parts, many appliances, furniture, etc.

The first thing Jeff did was he went down the list and selected every listing that had a phone number on the post. He wrote down all of the phone numbers, then he proceeded to call them one by one and explain to them that he was in the business of scrap metal recycling. He informed them that he would like to come by and pick up any and all metals that they wanted to get rid of.

The second thing Jeff did was he went down the list of those who didn't leave their phone number or their contact information. He reached out to them through Craigslist in the form of an email. In his email he included his contact information with a detailed two-sentence description of the service he was providing.

Often he would notice a cross street or an address in the posting that would tell him the items were already out front, ready to be picked up. The post would say something like, "first come, first served" and "this post will be taken down when the item is gone," or something to that effect. Jeff would always pay attention to how old the posting was.

Jeff was smart. He knew that if the item had been listed early in the morning, and he happened to be looking at it later in the afternoon, then there was a good chance that the item might have already been taken. He wasn't about to drive all the way out there on a whim, only to find out the job had been completed already.

To prevent this from happening he would always establish some form of contact with the person who created the post to make sure that the item was still available before driving to the site. Jeff knew that it was best to stay on top of this, so he would get up early in the morning and check to see what new posts had come out. He would always try to contact the owner and get them to commit to him by establishing a time of arrival. Some of them would and some simply wouldn't, do to their past experiences with people not showing up. His goal was to get a commitment, but if he couldn't, he would at least communicate with them to let them know that he was on his way.

Jeff would always start with posts that had been made within the last 24 hours. He would call on older posts as well, but he knew that the odds were stacked more in his favor on posts that had been made within 24 hours. Once he went through all of those, he would check every hour to see if anything new had popped up. This is how Jeff would stay on top of Craigslist's free section and make sure he was always the first one there if possible.

Jeff was able to do this nearly every single day while he was getting his scrap hustle off the ground. He began leaving his phone number behind with the people he met on Craigslist and letting them know that they could call him anytime they had more metal to get rid of. He began turning one-time customers into repeat customers and things were running smoothly, until one day…

Jeff had noticed that another scrapper had been arriving at his stops before he did. This would happen with the customers who weren't willing to commit to Jeff and who kept it on a first come, first served basis. This bothered Jeff because it represented about half of his potential new prospects on Craigslist. In fact, as a scrapper, Jeff simply wasn't going to have it! He couldn't stand being beaten to the punch by anyone.

Jeff decided to sit down with a pen and a sketchpad and come up with a game plan. He realized that whoever this new character was, they were obviously willing to get up early and be there promptly, which meant to him that this person was probably just as hungry for the business as he was. This proposed a direct threat. It was time to get strategic.

Each time Jeff would arrive at a potential customer's home, only to realize that he had again lost out to the other scrapper, he decided that he would ask the customer why he had missed out on the scrap metal. He would ask what kind of truck the other guy was driving. Jeff would make it sound like he was curious to see if his business partner had gotten there before him, so that the customer wouldn't get uneasy about describing the vehicle for him.

After having this happen to him a number of times, he was able to determine that it had been the exact same vehicle who was simply getting to the job before him.

What Jeff decided to do was start waking up earlier in the morning. He also discovered that he could download Craigslist as a mobile app on his cell phone. This enabled him to start checking on new postings by clicking the refresh button on the Craigslist mobile app every 15 minutes so he would get an update on anything new that was posted. Before this he would check his computer every hour and sometimes every 30 minutes or so.

Jeff was a competitive guy and for him to know that

somebody else was beating him to the punch consistently was simply unacceptable. Within Jeff, a new type of competitive, entrepreneurial, and dirty-boxing type of a scrapper would emerge!

Jeff was savvy and he thrived on competition. Not only did Jeff begin to check his phone every 15 minutes to ensure that he saw every new posting as it came out, but he also had another trick up his sleeve. Jeff knew that his competitor had been watching Craigslist like a hawk as well. He also knew that his competitor had been responding quickly to everybody who was posting as "first come, first served." Jeff knew that he would never drive more than 15 miles out of his way to pick up a small amount of metal because it wouldn't have been cost effective to him if he didn't get the scrap. He would only drive that sort of distance for metal that was going to make him $60 or more for one stop—especially with it being on a first come, first served posting.

Jeff decided to take a drive down to his local scrapyard. He got permission to take some photos with his phone for a nonexistent "homework assignment" that he'd been working on for his nonexistent "photography class." He found a pile of steel near the bottom of a large stockpile at the scrapyard. The pile he took a picture of represented about two tons of prepared iron. At the time this was valued at around $400.

The pictures that he took were perfect; he didn't make it obvious they were taken at a scrapyard because they were taken close up. He also took several pictures of the aluminum rims, the electric motors, radiators, car batteries, and large piles of sheet metal. He took multiple photos of each from different angles. He would also rearrange the positioning of the items so that it looked like they were in completely different settings.

Later that evening, when Jeff got home, he took the photos that had been taken from multiple angles, and had them strategically spaced out and staged. He now had 14 different photos which appeared to be taken from 14 different locations. It was time for Jeff to start fighting dirty! Jeff was in the scrap game and he was going to win at all costs.

He knew that most people, including himself, would at least take Sunday off from scrapping, which would make Monday the busiest day for picking up scrap that was posted for free on Craigslist. This was simply because Monday would be backed up with Sunday's postings because most scrapyards were closed on Sundays and most scrappers wouldn't work on Sundays anyway. So Monday would have its own new postings, but Sunday would usually be untouched.

Around 6 a.m. Monday morning, Jeff made his first post on Craigslist in the free section with roughly two tons of scrap metal located about 20 miles out of his town. This represented about $400 worth of scrap metal based on his market conditions. He got onto Google maps and picked an area that appeared to be somewhere that was likely to have a lot of dirt roads and large properties. He posted a single picture of a pile of prepared iron on a "first come, first served" basis.

He left no phone number and stated in his post that the post would be removed as soon as the job was completed. He even included a description of the cross streets nearest to the job, along with special instructions of how to find the correct dirt road to turn down. His post was very detailed with specific road markers, such as the "red mailbox that sets back off the main road about 30 feet," or "the green swinging gate out front about three miles" after the cross streets given in the post.

Of course, none of these reference points actually existed. Jeff's goal was to send his main competitors as far out of town as possible for his Monday harvest of scrap metal that had been backed up since Sunday. He would even get email notifications from people through Craigslist which were completely anonymous. This was because Craigslist would intercept the email and transfer the email from one user to another without revealing any specific email address. These emails would be about how they couldn't find the driveway. At that point he wouldn't respond to them, he would just wait for about 30 minutes, and then remove the free posting from Craigslist. He knew this would set his competitors back about two hours between the drive time to get to the nonexistent location, the searching upon arrival for the nonexistent driveway, the confusion, and lag time that they had trying to figure out where this mysterious pile of steel was located. Not to mention their drive home and fuel expenses.

Jeff knew this gave him a two-hour window of opportunity to secure and show up first to all the backed up Sunday postings, as well as the new Monday postings. Especially the ones that were listed as "first come, first served." This left the playing field wide open for Jeff and him alone! With more than one of his competitors roughly two hours behind what was going on locally, Jeff was able to clean house! He was able to do it on the most profitable day for free pick-ups on Craigslist in his local area.

Jeff would do this on a regular basis and then remove his post. This continued to work like a dream for him because there was no way to trace this back to him as long as he removed the post. With this being a "first come, first served" type of a post—stating that the post would be taken down when service was no longer needed—although confusing, it looked legitimate to his competitors when the post was removed. Jeff just assumed that most of his competitors probably moved on, assuming that somebody else got there first.

Between refreshing his phone every 15 minutes, waking up early, as well as sending his competitors on a wild goose chase every once in a while, this is how Jeff eventually dominated the free section of Craigslist with his scrap metal removal service.

This concludes the story of Jeff and how he got the most out of Craigslist, without *ever* having to spend money on advertising!

Lesson 13

Joe's Gorilla Marketing Story Using Craigslist

In this example, Craigslist Method #2, we are going to use Joe's flyer and business card. Joe's strategy was to re-purpose his card or flyer to be used digitally. In the following example, you will learn how Joe used his digital business card to pass out across the Internet through Craigslist.

Joe used his smartphone to take a perfectly aligned picture of his business card. He didn't turn his phone sideways, just straight up and down with his business card laying on a flat surface with a solid background. He took a picture of the business card with as little of the background as possible. He wanted it to look presentable as he would be emailing this as well as texting this business card to several people who had placed ads on Craigslist and other areas of the Internet.

Now, before he did this, there was one caveat that made it work. He would always ask "permission" to send his information to a number of people who were listed on Craigslist. Below is an example of how Joe worded his request for permission:

"Hello, my name is Joe Blow with Joe Blow's Scrap Metal Removal Service. I noticed your ad on Craigslist. I can be reached at 1-800-JOE-BLOW. I am a local resident and I would like to send you a flyer or business card with a list of metals that I take completely free of charge with same-day service. If this would serve you or your business, please let me know and I'll get my information right over to you."

Joe was smart about it and got straight to the point. At that moment, Joe had already delivered his name and phone number while asking permission to send them his flyer. This is how he would sneak into their text logs or email archives where they could go back and find his information at any time. This way even if they said no, Joe didn't have permission, they would still have his name and phone number stored in their archives in case the need for his service were to arise in the future.

If somebody told him not to spam them, he would simply say that he wouldn't reach out to them again, thank them anyway, and move on.

Joe knew that it was possible for somebody to potentially report him to Craigslist as a spammer. Joe also knew that if this happened, Craigslist could potentially put his account on hold, making it impossible for him to continue marketing his services in this particular fashion. Joe was not concerned with this at all because he realized that all he would have to do was create a new email and use a different phone number in order to get a new account.

Joe understood this rarely happened; however, if it did happen he was prepared to get a burner phone and create a new Yahoo Mail account. This would have him back up and running within a couple hours. If Craigslist happened to recognize his IP address, then he would go take care of it at the public library or on a friend's computer.

Joe was aware of the fact that being reported was possible, but he had done this multiple times in the past and never had an issue. The one thing Joe never did was just send his business card without asking for "permission." Based on his past experience, Joe knew that if he were to be lazy and just send a plain old picture of his business card, he would be viewed as spam immediately.

In Joe's experience, he had always gotten the most favorable results by asking permission first, while sneaking his phone number and name in there at the same time. If the prospect happened to say, "Yes, sure, go ahead and send me your flyer," then Joe would immediately follow up with another picture of his flyer with all the metals that he accepted, just like he did with the business card. He would then thank them for their interest and let them know he looked forward to hearing from them.

Joe used this method to open up the lines of communication with a wide array of businesses via email or text message. These businesses included: contractors, electricians, plumbers, demolition contractors, HVAC contractors, mechanics, solar companies, auto body repair shops, realtors, property managers, tire repair shops, equipment repair shops, towing companies, appliance stores, appliance repair stores, tire and rim stores, CNC machine shops, foundries, fencing companies, patio installation companies, handymen, etc.

Where Joe was located geographically, there were two counties within his reach that were neighboring the county he lived in. He realized that it made sense for him to start from home first. This was most cost-effective for his travel expenses and his travel time.

Once Joe had reached out to everybody in his town and county, he would move over to the next city closest to him and repeat this process. He would begin reaching out to all the tradesmen and business owners who advertised in the services section and small business section of Craigslist, as well as other businesses on

Google. Sometimes Joe would get no response at all, sometimes he was told no, sometimes he got instant results, but what was important to Joe were the results he did get.

Joe realized that just because some gave him no response at all, that didn't mean they told him no. Nor did they say yes. To Joe it stood to reason that maybe they'd overlooked his flyer or his business card. Joe resolved to create a list of all his prospects who didn't tell him no or to stop contacting them. He excluded the ones who did and he excluded the ones who had already given him favorable results. He repeated this process on a monthly basis, generally around the middle of the month.

Joe understood, based on his experience, that most business owners were sweating bullets toward the end of the month. Usually between the 28th through the 5th of the next month because that was when they would have to pay for the largest portion of their overhead: their rent or their mortgage in their business and personal life, if not both at the same time.

He knew not to reach out to them during this period of time because they were usually stressed out about paying all their bills on time. He didn't want to be the guy who sent them something they weren't expecting during a time when they were already a little agitated.

Joe always waited until he was sure the majority of them had paid their bills and were in the process of rebounding financially from the beginning of the month. This is why he would always reach out around the 10th and the 20th or so every month. Joe would always go back through his list and repeat this process until he got some sort of a response. He would document his results and then repeat the process. Joe did this until his list became clear as to who was interested in his service and who wasn't.

With Joe having an established list, excluding all of those who were not interested, his list was comprised of multiple interested tradesmen, business owners, retailers, and the like. The first thing he did was build a schedule that ran from Monday through Saturday. Joe would schedule his new clients with a two-hour window of estimated time of arrival, or an ETA for short. Joe would simply ask what day of the week best fit their schedule. He would also let them know about his time window system, and allow them to pick which window of time worked best for them based on his availability.

Some told him to come anytime; some gave him specific times. However, with Joe's scheduling system in place, he was able to accommodate almost anything.

This concludes Joe's strategy for making money with Craigslist for free.

In the next lessons you will learn about simple and easy ways to use and make inexpensive business cards, flyers, and door hangers so that you can also emulate Joe's strategy. If you are brand new to this, I would highly suggest understanding this process because you will be needing them for the rest of your career as an entrepreneur.

Note: If you are already familiar with how to produce business cards, flyers, and door hangers, feel free to skip these next two lessons and move on to the story of Ted and his paid ad strategy with Craigslist.

Lesson 14

How to Effectively Use Business Cards, Flyers, and Door Hangers

This lesson is important because you'll want to have these things prepared before you start placing ads online or anywhere else. You can do without these things, but it's best to have them in order to maximize your profits.

For example, let's say that you receive a phone call from a customer who has picked up one of your ads, either online or offline. You answer the phone correctly, you establish rapport with the customer, and you secure the job. You go to the customer's house and you load their unwanted metals. They are happy with what you have done and you have made a profit.

Why let your moneymaking end here? There are steps that you can take to dramatically increase the amount of money you make with each customer, if you have business cards in your pocket. Having flyers in your truck, car, van, or whatever you're driving is even better. I'll explain why door hangers are important as well. In the following examples you will learn a couple strategies to increase your profitability with the use of business cards, flyers, and door hangers.

Business Cards

Imagine you have arrived at your customer's home or business and completed scrap metal removal services for your customer. Before you get back in your vehicle, always make sure to hand your customer three business cards: one for them to keep, one for them to lose, and one for them to give to a friend, relative, or neighbor.

Word of mouth is going to be your ultimate moneymaker. However, if your customer has nothing to remember you by, such as a business card or flyer, then they have no way to pass your information on to the next person.

Always make sure to leave your customer with your contact information—preferably business cards. If you run out of business cards, leave them a flyer. This will enable your existing customers to find you and generate repeat business for you. It will also enable your customers to pass along your information to friends, family, and neighbors.

Flyers and Door Hangers

You have completed a scrap metal removal service for your customer. The customer is very happy with your service. You've already handed him three business cards and you are about ready to leave the property. Whether you're at a business or a residence, it is highly likely that your customer has some kind of a relationship with their neighbors. Next-door neighbors are often on a first name basis. Here is how you can use it to your advantage.

After you've established that your customer is satisfied with your service, ask your customer if they think either one of their adjacent neighbors would benefit from a free scrap metal removal service on their property since you're already in the area. Often, your customer will be more than willing to walk over, knock on the door, and ask them personally on your behalf. They may even call or text their neighbors as well. This is your first attempt at reaching out to your customer's neighbors, while essentially turning your customer into your temporary salesperson.

If your customer shows no indication they are going to reach out to their neighbors on your behalf, then that's okay. It doesn't happen every time. In fact, probably less than half of your customers will do this. However, when they do, it can and has turned into a gold mine for many scrappers.

This is where flyers come into play. You can ask your customer what their neighbors' names are. You'll tell your customer that you're going to walk over and see if you can assist the neighbors in providing them with free scrap metal removal service, since you're already next door to their house.

If you're the type of person to walk up and knock on somebody's door and be willing to talk to them, it will be most effective. However, there's another way to approach this as well. Below are two scenarios of what you can do with flyers, whether you knock on the door or not.

Flyer Scenario 1

You've knocked on the door and the neighbor answers. You let them know right away that you are not a salesman. Usually you will see a sense of relief in the neighbor's demeanor. You then proceed to tell the neighbor that you were just next door at their neighbor, "Mike's" house, doing a free metal removal and disposal service for him.

Reiterate the fact that your service is completely free of charge and that you're simply stopping by to see if you can help get rid of some unwanted clutter in their garage or around their property. At this point, you'll hand Mike's neighbor your flyer and point him toward the list of excepted materials toward the middle of your flyer. Explain that there are items missing from the list to save space on your flyer.

Inform the neighbor that if they have a question about an item not on the list that you'd be happy to take a look at it. Let the neighbor know they can keep your flyer in case they have any family, friends, or relatives that may be in need of your service. In that moment, you're either going to make money instantly, or, at the very least, you have planted a seed that may grow into a phone call for you in the future.

If you are not comfortable with knocking on somebody's door and speaking to them at their home, that's okay; you may be more comfortable with the approach in this next scenario.

Flyer Scenario 2

After you've received the names of the neighbors, you'll want to go back to your vehicle, or someplace where you can sit down, and write a couple of sentences. This is when having door hangers (a type of flyer that hooks around a doorknob or handle) will come in very handy!

Let's say the neighbor's name is Manuel. You will want to fold your standard flyer in half (like a tent) and address the neighbor by his first name, as if you were writing a letter to a friend. You will essentially right down everything you would have said in Scenario 1, but with a bit of a twist. Below is an example of how your message should appear:

Manuel!

Sorry we missed you! Your neighbor, Mike, had us come out today to declutter his property of unwanted metal items. The service was completely free of charge. If you need us, we're here for you. Our contact info is listed on the other side. Feel free to call or text anytime!

Thanks,

Joe Blow's Scrap Metal Removal.

You will simply leave the folded flyer on the neighbor's doorstep or hang it on their door handle, anywhere visible. This will be more effective than a generic flyer because it is *addressed* to Manuel. It is handwritten and there is mention of his neighbor already having used your service.

Lesson 15

How to Create Inexpensive Business Cards, Flyers, and Door Hangers

Here we're going to talk about a couple of inexpensive ways to have these marketing tools made so that you're prepared to double down on your profits when you get to a customer's house.

Business Cards

A strong resource for business cards is The UPS Store. Generally, at any UPS store you can walk right in, tell them what you would like to have them print up, and they have packages to make your business cards, flyers, door hangers, and mailers.

There are also multiple resources out there online where you can accomplish this for a cheaper price. A couple of great online resources I recommend are www.vistaprint.com as well as www.zazzle.com. With these resources, it is important to know that most likely you'll be doing the design work yourself and placing the order yourself, if you choose to shop online. Therefore, you will be responsible for the results upon arrival of the product, warts and all.

I prefer The UPS Store because it's a one-stop shop. If you don't feel comfortable ordering your own business cards off the internet just yet, then this is a good place to start. For now, I am going to point you toward The UPS Store because there is usually one in every town or city.

At The UPS Store you can have your business cards made relatively cheap. I'm talking about a stack of 500-1000 business cards for around $20-$100 depending on how extravagant your design work is going to be. They will usually charge you a one-time design fee, so be ready to pay that. At the time this book was written the design fee was around $60. The cost of business cards and design fees may fluctuate depending on when you happen to read this book.

Don't get me wrong, if you ask for a Picasso level of artwork on your business card, then the design fee will most likely go up as well as the cost to print your cards. For what you are doing I would suggest that you keep it simple. Start out with the most basic black and white business card as possible, if you want to save money. If you have a little extra cash, then I would recommend using two different fonts and two different colors.

What's great about The UPS Store is that they have business card templates and formats already laid out for you. All you have to do is pick and choose the template that you would like to have appear on your business card. After you've made your selection they will do a mock up for you. This may take a little time, usually a day or two. Generally, they will send a sample to your email so that you can view it before they print them for you. If you don't have an email, then just leave your phone number with them and have them call you to come in and view their samples in person. The system they have in place totally streamlines the process and takes the stress out of having to create your own card.

To sum it up, I would recommend walking in there and telling the cashier what you're looking for. Somebody might come out of the back who is in charge of design, or the cashier may be equipped to handle that as well. Either way, I would tell them what you're trying to accomplish. Let them know what name you would like to have on your card (your first and last name would be sufficient), followed by "scrap metal removal service." Make sure your phone number is on there and if you have an email, make sure it's on there too. Tell them you want a black and white business card, nothing extravagant, just straight to the point. Finally, let them know you trust in their ability to design a business card.

Note: This is a relationship you will want to build as well. Be nice to the people at The UPS Store because it could be the difference between you getting pushed to the front of the line when you run out of flyers or business cards, or having to wait days or even weeks.

At this point, you'll probably hear something like this: "Well, we have design templates for you to choose from. If you have a minute, I can show you a few of them and let you pick which format you would like."

Go through that process with them and just pick one. If you're not sure which one will be the most effective, don't worry about it, you just need something to hand to your customers. You can always improve your design later. For now, we're going to get you up and running with business cards to hand to each customer that you serve. Getting your business cards back could take as little as three days up to three weeks depending on demand. Just be patient and soon you will have 500-1000 business cards ready to distribute.

Flyers and Door Hangers

It's virtually the same exact process here. They will have templates and formats already laid out for you to choose from. If The UPS Store that you happen to go to doesn't have templates ready for you, then ask them to see some samples of other work they have produced so you can mimic another flyer. Generally, they will have a template for you to choose from. All you will have to do is decide which one you like the best. With flyers, I would recommend you spend a little bit more money on these. I suggest you stick to no more than two colors and two fonts. Don't let me make this sound complicated, because it isn't. Just tell them what you're doing and give them your information, your name, phone number, and email if you have one. The email is not necessary for what you're trying to accomplish, but it does make you look more professional. Once again, they'll usually get back to you within a day or two with a sample, especially if you keep your design simple. Your design should be simple and straight to the point. Below is an example of a simple flyer that is straight to the point.

JOE BLOW'S SCRAP METAL REMOVAL

1-800-JOE-BLOW

We are a free scrap metal removal service!

Items that we accept:

- Appliances
- Barbecues
- Bicycles
- Brass

- fixtures/faucets
- Car parts
- Rims
- Copper tubing
- Copper wire
- Metal tubing
- Heavy iron
- Old trampolines
- Workout equipment
- Dumbbells/barbells & free weights
- Treadmills
- Patio furniture
- Metal decorations, including lamps

We can take anything that is considered 75% made of metal or greater!

If you have any questions about accepted items, please feel free to give us a call or text at 1-800-JOE-BLOW.

Call or text us today for a hassle free, no obligation consult!

There you have it folks! The example above is how simple and straight to the point one of your flyers should look. Again, you can get as creative as you want, nobody is stopping you. Flyers are more effective if you're able to add pictures instead of an itemized list, but an itemized list will work to get you started. Flyers with pictures will be more expensive, but also more effective. I would recommend spending more money on your flyers by using pictures, if you can. If it's not in your budget, don't worry, you will get plenty of responses just using text.

What's great about flyers and door hangers is that you can repurpose the content. Refer to the example above for your door hangers as well. The information can all stay the same and they will have a format for you to choose from with your door hanger selection as well. With door hangers, you can pretty much use them the same as you would a flyer. After you have reached out to the neighbors, it never hurts to hit every door on the street while you're already in the neighborhood. Or at least the five houses surrounding your customer's home. This example of how to use flyers, business cards, and door hangers has given you three ways of exposing your business while responding to one customer's phone call.

To conclude these lessons about business cards, flyers, and door hangers I would suggest you literally take this section of your book into The UPS Store or wherever you choose to have printing done. Show them the example illustrated above. Have them replace Joe Blow's name with your own. Then have them replace his phone number with yours. If you do this, you'll have an effective flyer in short order, and Joe Blow won't mind at all.

This concludes the lessons on business cards, flyers, and door hangers.

In the next lesson you will learn about "Ted's" journey with Craigslist and how he made his phone ring like crazy with inexpensive Craigslist ads. Pay very close attention to this lesson and really implement the strategies. Pay attention because what you'll learn in the following lesson could be responsible for a dramatic increase in your ability to make money with scrap metal recycling.

Lesson 16

Ted and His Craigslist Advertising Strategy

First of all, Craigslist has received a bad rap over the years when it comes to questionable services and shady deals. It's true there have been a lot of unfortunate things that have taken place as a result of a purchase or service provider on Craigslist. Now that we've gotten that out of the way, Craigslist can be a powerhouse for you if you go about it in the right way. It can help you hit the ground running hard and fast.

Once you've established a Craigslist account with an email and a username and password connected to a phone number, you are now able to post your ads on Craigslist through their many categories. You will only really need to deal with one category to maximize your results. Don't get me wrong, you will want to dominate this category by placing more ads up than anybody else.

This book is published in the year 2022. A few years prior to this, Craigslist used to allow posting free advertising in the services section, which is where you're going to be posting your ads as well. Now, if you're like Ted in the example below, you took full advantage of this, along with everybody else who wanted to hustle their hearts out and maximize their profits. You see, Craigslist previously allowed posting two ads per day, per account for free. So what this meant was that if you had six accounts, you could post 12 ads per day, absolutely free of charge. All you needed was an email account attached to a phone number, as well as a username and password, and you were "in like Flynn."

For this example, we are going to use a scrap hustler named Ted. Ted was ambitious and he wanted to make as much money as he possibly could quickly. He decided that he was going to apply all of the methods from this book to make them all work together for him. Ted was smart. He understood the value of free and cheap advertising.

What Ted did in the beginning, when Craigslist was still free and easy to take advantage of, was he got on Yahoo mail and created six different email accounts. They were his first and last name, followed by the number 1@yahoo.com, then followed by the number 2@yahoo.com, and then 3@yahoo.com, and so on and so forth until he had six. Of course, Ted needed six phone numbers to coincide with the six Yahoo email accounts because it was required by Craigslist for each new account. So what he did was he used his personal cell phone number for his first account, his wife's cell phone number for his second account, his daughter's for his third account, his son's for his fourth account, his mother-in-law for his fifth account, and one of his best friend's for his sixth account.

He let each one of them know that Craigslist was going to send them a verification code, and he needed them to send it back to him so that he could plug it into his laptop computer to activate the new account. He used the exact same password for all six accounts so he wouldn't forget if he was ever asked to provide the password. This kept things simple for Ted.

Once Ted was all set up with his six accounts, it was time for him to create ads. Now, he had never done this before. He wasn't exactly sure how to properly structure an ad on Craigslist. One day, after some trial and error, he created a decent ad with his information on it. Right as he was about to submit his ad to Craigslist and have it posted, he had an epiphany. He thought: *Why don't I go into the "labor and moving" section of Craigslist, find other people who have ads in my category, and see what they have done?*

Ted did exactly that. He got on Craigslist, went to the "labor and moving" section of Craigslist, then he clicked on it. When the next search engine was available, he typed in "scrap metal removal," and clicked on "search." He was astonished to see there were about 30 different people who were listed in this category. So what he did to save himself time and stress was he went through and figured out which ad had been posted the most frequently. He did this by clicking on the ad and figuring out the phone number that was listed on the ad. The reason he did this was because of the fact that the one who had been posting the most, for the longest period of time, was likely to be the most experienced. It was also highly probable he was getting good results from his ad if he was willing to repost the same exact one so many times consecutively.

To create an ad for himself, all Ted did was literally click on the ad and hit "copy" with the right click of his mouse. Then he dragged it over to his own posting that he was creating and right clicked again on his mouse and selected "paste." He reverse engineered a few sentences, rearranged some of the keywords, and replaced his phone number and contact information. This took Ted less than 10 minutes. He then had a highly effective ad ready to be posted, which is exactly what he did moments later. In fact, he spent about a total of 30 minutes dropping 12 ads in a row, one after another. Within six hours of his 12 posts in a row escapade, he had received three phone calls and secured two jobs.

Ted continued on like this for about a week. He thought: *How could I make this more effective?* Then he had another epiphany. Ted had previously spent a lot of his lifetime working as an employee. He had worked that 9-to-5 until he couldn't take it anymore. He reasoned that a good percentage of employees were all on the same schedule at any given time. This was evident to him based on morning traffic on his way to work. Ted also considered 5 o'clock traffic on his way home from work. He realized that he was likely in the same boat as everybody else at the time when he was working 9 to 5.

Ted knew that when he went to work he clocked in at 9 a.m., he was given a 15-minute break around 10:45, and a one-hour lunch break at 12:00 p.m. He was given another 15-minute break at 2 and then finally was allowed to go home at 5 p.m. Ted knew that based on his typical behavior as an employee, that he would never have time during work hours to search for anything on his own personal phone or computer.

Ted figured this was probably true for everybody else as well. However, he also knew that before he had to go to work, before he left his house for example, he spent a little time on his computer or on his phone, either on social media or solving non-work related problems, such as paying bills, shopping, etc. He also knew that as soon as he got his one-hour lunch break, it was usually accompanied by time on his cell phone. This also took place on his 15-minute break a couple hours later. Then, after his one-hour drive home from work, dinner, and a shower, he and his family usually found themselves staring at some sort of mobile device by about 7:00 p.m.

With this in mind he came to a conclusion. Ted decided that instead of posting 12 ads in a row during a 30-minute time window, once per day, he would instead spread out the volume of posts throughout the course of the day, in order to make sure his ads were going up around the time he expected people to have their cell phones in their hands or laptop in front of them. He figured that his ad would already have been buried by other ads if he continued doing them all at once.

So what Ted did was he posted two ads between the hours of 7 and 8 in the morning. He posted two more ads between 10 and 11 in the morning. He posted two more ads between 12 and 1 in the afternoon. Then, he posted two ads between 2 and 3 in the afternoon, and two more between 6 and 7. Finally, his last two ads he would post at 8 p.m. because he reasoned that between 9 and 10 might be a little too late for people who have to get up and go to work early in the morning.

Ted wanted to catch people when they were most likely to have their phones in their hands and be browsing online. This worked like magic for him. He realized, after tracking his phone calls and his numbers for a month, that this method was 100% more effective than his old method. Ted did this for over two years and everything was working beautifully. He was making money hand over fist, picking up new customers almost every day, and turning them into clients who in some cases called him regularly for service.

One early summer morning, Ted woke up ready to attack his day and start slaying dragons out in the streets as usual, when he was suddenly met with an obstacle that would change the course of his career in an instant. The year was 2018 when Ted opened up his first Craigslist account and couldn't gain access to it. He had a message from Craigslist saying that his account had been suspended. He thought: *That's strange.* So he opened up his second Craigslist account. This account was suspended as well. He opened his third, his fourth, his fifth, and his sixth account and they were all suspended. He didn't know what to think. He wasn't sure if he had done something wrong and he just couldn't get Craigslist on the phone no matter how hard he tried.

So he resolved to create another user name and password and asked another friend of his to use their phone number so that he could activate a new account.

Fortunately for Ted, his friend was willing. He was able to activate his new account. He had saved a copy of his old ad by taking a picture of it with his phone and sending it to his email after he had initially created it. All he had to do was retype the ad exactly how it appeared in the picture that he took in order to recreate the exact same ad.

He looked it over, clicked "submit post," and to his surprise a new screen he had never seen before popped up in front of him after he clicked on the submit post. Ted was astonished when he learned that Craigslist was now going to be charging $5 per post, for every post in the "labor and moving" section. At first he was floored by this! He started doing some math and quickly realized this was going to cost him $60 per day.

This meant that Ted would need to begin spending $1,440 per month for advertising space that had previously been free to him less than 24 hours prior. Ted had been posting six days per week. If he wanted to keep posting at this rate, he had a major decision to make!

Now, Ted knew Craigslist was highly effective and this could take a serious chunk out of his monthly income, if he were to continue running ads at this pace. After thinking about it and doing his own personal cost-benefit analysis, Ted realized something. He realized that if he stopped running ads at this rate, he stood to lose a lot more than $1,440 per month. He also believed if he continued running ads at this pace, he would have about the same amount of income. It was just going to cost him now to generate that income. However, Ted was a thinker.

Ted determined that this was going to mean a lot of people who had previously been advertising for free in his category on Craigslist were probably not going to see the value of paying for something that was previously free to them. He realized this because one of his mentors, when he was younger, used to have a saying that went something like this: "luxuries once tasted become necessities." Ted thought: *If that's true, then all of these so-called competitors of mine who are completely drunk on the taste of free Craigslist advertising are more than likely not going to want to pay the heavy price that Craigslist is asking for high-volume ad posting.*

Ted was almost certain that a large percentage of them would abandon posting on Craigslist all together. He rationalized that if that happened, then only those who were willing to pay would be getting a greater percentage of the Craigslist phone traffic. He reasoned there would be less competition in the space, yet the same amount of demand for his service.

He came up with a theory that even if he didn't make

more money than he was making before, his income would increase at least enough to cover the cost of the ads. In turn, this would increase the amount of repeat customers that he didn't have to spend money on to get their business afterward. Which in turn would increase his clientele base because it would open up more opportunities for him to pass out business cards, door hangers, and flyers as well. Ted believed all of these things would work together for him in the long run.

At this point, Ted had a decision to make. Would he back off on advertising, stop advertising, or keep advertising at the same rate? Ted had an entrepreneurial spirit and a thirst for risk-taking. He decided to keep his advertising the exact same and pay the $60 per day. He decided he would give this a 30-day trial and close monitoring. He noted how many calls he received every day, how much income he made every day, as well as how many other competitors were posting each day in comparison to before when Craigslist was allowing free ad postings.

It took Ted no less than two weeks to realize his hunch was 100% correct. By the end of the first week, after analyzing the data, he realized his income had increased by around 25%, as well as his incoming calls. Ted also realized, after going through and counting the number of ads, as well as the number of phone numbers listed on those ads, that the number of people placing ads on Craigslist in his particular section where he posted had gone down by a considerable amount. In addition to that he realized some of his strongest competitors—meaning those who had previously been posting almost as frequently as him—had reduced the amount of ads they were posting, in some cases by 50% or even more.

What changed about Craigslist at that time for Ted was now he didn't have to go through all the trouble of going in and opening six different accounts to post and repost throughout his day. Craigslist simply wanted $5 per posting and it wasn't necessary to operate off more than one account. Which meant all he had to do was open his Craigslist mobile app on his cell phone every two hours and repost two of his ads with the click of a button. This actually simplified the process for Ted. Because Ted was tracking his numbers meticulously, he realized in the second week more of his competitors had either decreased their ads or stopped completely.

Ted was now two weeks into the 30-day trial he had committed to when he had another epiphany. Ted realized his income had gone up by another 10% compared to the previous week and that he had changed nothing about the number of ads he posted. He rationalized that because his income was going up and his competitors were going away, he would continue to hold this pattern until his income, as well as his incoming calls, hit a plateau and leveled out. He even thought about adding one more ad every two hours, bringing the total up to 16 per day. He was going to do this to take a risk and to take up more real estate in the "labor and moving" ads section of Craigslist for visibility purposes. However, he didn't want to be irrational and pull the trigger too early without seeing what kind of results he could get from what he was already spending.

So Ted decided to hold his current pattern of spending. Over the next three months, Ted's income increased week after week and month after month, until he finally hit his plateau and his strongest competitors began to increase the amount of ads they were posting. Ted realized they had probably noticed how many ads he was posting and how consistently he was doing it, so they decided they needed to start matching him in order to compete with him.

At this point his numbers had leveled out; they were steady, but they weren't rapidly increasing any longer. Ted was okay with this because the amount of repeat customers he had acquired during that three-month window of time, when everybody else got lazy and too scared to spend money, would serve him for years to come. He knew he had set the bar for what was required to compete with him using paid Craigslist ads in his local section.

Ted would go back and forth with competitors. If somebody would increase their spending to three ads every two hours, he would do four. This would make things really expensive for everybody. Finally, when the dust settled and the ad war stopped, everybody was averaging between 10 and 12 ads per day.

This is how Ted overcame the adversity of Craigslist charging money for what he was used to utilizing them for free of charge. In the process of overcoming this adversity, Ted dominated and set the bar for what was necessary to compete for the lion's share of the real estate in his local Craigslist "labor and moving" section.

If Ted were to start brand new on Craigslist today, he would start by posting one Craigslist ad between 7 and 8 in the morning. He would post again between 12 and 1 in the afternoon, and another between 6 and 7 in the evening. He would do this to get cash rolling in as fast as possible. Once the phone started ringing, he would then apply the principles outlined in this book in the next lesson, about how to answer the phone and close the deal. He would realize profits daily.

Ted wouldn't spend all the money he earned on things he didn't need. Instead, he would take as much of his profit as possible, if not all of it, and he would double down on his advertising budget. He would repeat this process until he got up to around 12 ads per day, then he would maintain this amount of posting permanently.

It is much easier for Ted now that he doesn't have to have six Craigslist accounts and jump through all those hoops. Now he can simply have one phone number attached to one email address and use one credit card or debit card to pay for as many ads as he would like.

This concludes the story of "Ted" and his inexpensive ways of dominating Craigslist using paid ads.

It's one thing to know how to make your phone ring with advertising and marketing. However, it is equally important to know what to say and do after you answer the phone. Our next lesson is a short and easy to digest example of how to conduct yourself once you've gotten your phone to ring.

Lesson 17

How to Answer the Phone Correctly and What Questions to Ask

I want to get you prepared for what happens when your phone actually begins to ring. My goal is to get you prepared for what to say to your customers initially and how to respond to them. You can generate all the inbound phone calls you want; however, if you don't have a few basic tools in your tool belt you won't stand a chance on the phone. In this lesson you'll read an example of a typical customer phone call who is looking for a scrap metal removal service.

Imagine, your phone rings…you answer it. Now, you could just say hello and the conversation will likely continue, sounding something like this: "Hi, I saw one of your ads. I just want to make sure I've got the right number. Do you guys pick up scrap metal from people's homes?"

We will continue on into how to respond to the customer after I make this short point. You can remove the element of concern and shorten the communication process if you answer the phone in the fashion laid out in the scenario below.

In this example you will see how Matt answers his phone calls professionally, as well as how he conducts his conversations.

Matt's phone rings.

Matt answers, "Hi! Thank you for calling Matt's Scrap Metal Removal Service. This is Matt, how may I help you today?"

This is basic customer service training. If you speak clearly and pleasantly with a tone in your voice that suggests you are ready to come right now and solve the customer's problem immediately, not only do you eliminate the element of concern that a customer has the wrong number, but you also qualify yourself as somebody who does this regularly and can be depended upon.

If you are just going to say hello, that's a little lazy, but it will work.

Let's assume that you picked up the phone the way Matt did. Matt answered the phone like a professional. His response back from the customer went something like this:

Customer: "Hi, I have a washer and dryer that have gone bad, a refrigerator, a couple of bikes, an old barbecue, and a treadmill that I would like to get rid of. Is that something you can take?"

Matt: "Absolutely, that is what I do for a living. How soon would you like to get on the schedule? I have room on my route today. Does today work for you?"

Note: This is Matt going straight for the kill. He doesn't leave it up to the customer to decide whether it's going to be next weekend or two weeks from now. No, Matt wants to let them know that he's available almost immediately, and he can work around their schedule anytime today. This is very suggestive language in order to let his customer know that he wants to come today. There's nothing wrong with this because most of the time the customer would like their old unwanted debris off their property as soon as possible. Asking if the customer would like service today is a strong attempt at placing less time between Matt and his money. The sooner Matt gets those items in his possession, the faster his personal wealth can start to grow.

In this example, we're going to assume the customer says yes.

Customer: "Yeah, today works for me! What time do you have available?"

Matt: "I can be there within an hour from right now. I will call you or send a text when I am 20 minutes away, so that you know exactly when I'll be there. Does that work for you?"

Customer: "That is perfect. I'll see you when you get here!"

Matt: "Sounds good! Also, one more thing. Where will everything be situated on your property? This helps me to decide what type of loading equipment I will need."

Customer: "I have some in the garage, and some of it is on the side of the house. There's a refrigerator on the back patio with a cement walkway on the side of the house where you can get to the back. If you have a dolly or something like that, you can easily wheel it down the walkway. In fact, I think it has wheels underneath because we rolled it to our back sliding glass door before we lifted it over and put it outside."

Matt: "That is no problem, everything sounds perfect to me. The more things that can be ready to go in one spot the better. Whatever is too difficult is no problem. Leave it up to me and I'll gladly take care of it for you. Now, if I could please get you to text me the address so I can put it in my GPS, I would really appreciate it. If you can't text, I can write it down, it's no problem."

Customer: "Great. I'll send it right now."

Matt: "Thank you so much! It was nice talking with you and I look forward to meeting you. I'll call ahead!"

Customer: "Thanks, same to you!"

Note: If Matt's customer hadn't wanted same day service, and the following day would have been better, then Matt would have simply taken down the customer's name, address, and phone number. He would have used a standard notepad, or set a reminder in his phone. He was aware that there is scheduling software out there, but he did the best he could with what he already had. Matt would simply write down his customer's name, phone number, and address, as well as the date they would like for him to provide service. He used two-hour time windows when scheduling jobs out into the future. Below is an example of Matt's time window schedule:

9:00 a.m. - 11:00 a.m.

11:00 a.m. - 1:00 p.m.

1:00 p.m. - 3:00 p.m.

3:00 p.m. - 5:00 p.m.

5:00 p.m. - 7:00 p.m.

You'll want to ask your customer which window of time would work best for them, then write it down or type it into your notes. Let the customer know you will follow up the evening before to confirm your appointment. Of course, you'll actually want to do this. Remember, people's plans change and yours will too at times, but when you make a commitment to a customer, do your best to get there on time. Also, just like in an earlier example, let the customer know that you will be calling or texting them 20 or 30 minutes ahead of time, before you show up so they know your exact ETA.

This is how you schedule an appointment with a customer. Not every customer is going to interact with you the same way. However, the example above is a typical phone call that you will receive. After some experience, you will see exactly why this is a good example.

Lesson 18

What to Do When You Arrive at the Customer's Home

What should you do when you arrive at your customer's home? What is the very first thing you should say? What is the very first action you should take? In this lesson we will get straight to the point. You will learn how to address your customer from the moment you get out of your vehicle in order to execute the deal properly. This is the simple and easy way to leave a good first impression with your customer. The old saying goes, "you don't get a second chance to make a first impression." I have found that to be true. So the way you approach your customers, from the time you pull up, get out, and make your initial introduction, is crucial.

First of all, like I mentioned in earlier lessons, it is important that, at the very least, your attire is clean and preferably ironed with no wrinkles. If you can get a collared shirt that's even better. Even if you have to go to a thrift store and spend $5 on a collared shirt or two. If you're wearing a hat, make sure it's on straight and do a mirror check before you hop out of the vehicle. Make sure that you look as professional and clean-cut as possible.

For this scenario we're going to use Brandon's example. Brandon was a bartender in the evenings. He worked at a nice restaurant serving drinks four nights per week. The hourly wage they were paying him was next to nothing. He was only hanging in there because he made so much money with his tips. On an average night he would make $60-$80 in tips. However, he was paid $10 per hour for his wages. Between both, he figured with tips and his hourly wage combined, he was bringing home around $20 per hour with an average shift being six hours. When he did his numbers he realized that on average every month he was making about $2,000 give or take.

Brandon realized his bills were about $1,600 a month, between his car payment, his rent, and his insurance. This left him very little at the end of each month for entertainment, food, or anything else. He decided he wanted to make a change, and he wanted to make a change happen fast.

Brandon knew he had all day long to figure something out because he worked in the evenings. He would usually go in to work around 8 in the evening, when things started to really pick up at the bar, and he would get off around 2 in the morning as the bar was shutting down. He would generally get seven or eight hours of sleep, then wake up between 10 and 11 in the morning.

Brandon was smart and he had ambition. He wanted to make more money, but he wasn't sure how to approach making money without another job. So one day before he went in to work, he got on the internet and started looking for ways to make money. After doing his online search he discovered the scrap metal recycling industry. He had never been exposed to the scrap metal recycling industry before and he was fascinated by how he could make cash quickly and daily, just like he did at his job. He stumbled across *How to Make Ca$h Today! with Scrap Metal Recycling* on Amazon's Kindle store. He read the e-book, downloaded the audiobook, and learned so much that he even purchased several of the hardcover copies to give all his friends and family for Christmas and birthdays. (Shameless plug LOL!)

After Brandon had answered the phone properly, using Matt's example laid out previously, he set the appointment and headed over to his very first customer's house. The first thing he did was make sure he took a look in the mirror as he was pulling up to the property. He checked his hair, teeth, nose, and made sure his collar looked nice. Also, right before he stepped out of his truck, he sprayed on a couple squirts of his favorite cologne; so not only would he look professional for his customer, but he would also smell good as he approached.

He made sure he remembered his customer's name was Bryson. It was easy to remember this because, as he was setting the appointment, the first question he asked was for his customer's name and address to put in his GPS, so he would know where he was going.

After putting on cologne and checking his appearance in the mirror, Brandon stepped out of the truck he had backed down Bryson's driveway with a big smile on his face, walking toward him with his hand out, ready for a handshake, and said, "You must be Bryson!"

Bryson responded to Brandon with a joke, "Well, at least for the last 35 years that's who I've been."

They both laughed and shook hands. This is when Brandon took control of the conversation and said to Bryson, "Okay, my friend, I understand you have some unwanted items on your property that are taking up space and you called me to solve that problem for you."

Bryson responded to Brandon, "Yes sir, I do."

Taking a step forward, walking toward Bryson's property as if to say with his body language, *Let's go take a look,* Brandon replied, "I'll follow you, just point it out and it's coming with me!"

As they walked around the side of the house, Bryson went on pointing out an old refrigerator, as well as a washer and dryer on his side yard. These were taking up space and he couldn't park his boat in the backyard because of them. He also showed Brandon a set of old aluminum rims. He went on to the back of his house where he pointed out an old bumper, some steel fencing, and miscellaneous car parts such as rotors, brake pads, nuts, and bolts.

At this point, Bryson told Brandon this was pretty much everything he wanted to get rid of and he even offered to give Brandon a hand. Brandon jokingly said, "Well yeah, I'll take free help anyway I can get it." They laughed and started right from the back of the house where they were standing, dragging everything to the front and loading it onto Brandon's truck. From that day forward, every time Bryson needed any scrap metal removed from his home, Brandon was his go-to guy.

This concludes the example of how Brandon approached his customer after arriving at his house.

Congratulations! You have now completed Part 2 of this book on how to make cash today with scrap metal recycling.

Part Three

Introduction

Congratulations yet again on your decision to step your game up by increasing your entrepreneurial IQ through self-education. You couldn't have learned this in school even if they tried to teach it. This is simply because it's coming from the school of hard knocks. This is the type of knowledge that can only be gained by experience through many years of trial and error. It is my honor to have taken a decade of experience and condensed it into a three-part book that you, the reader, can use to hopefully change your life immediately and improve your future for many years to come. In Part 3 you will be given examples of how to become more efficient as well as how to go after small business accounts. Now, with the introduction out of the way, let's go!

Lesson 19

How Nathan Differentiated Himself from His Competition

We're going to take a brief look at the moving company, PODS, compared to another moving company, Two Men And A Truck. You're going to see how it is possible to take a position in an industry that is the opposite of what your competitors are doing, and be extremely competitive by being more efficient about the services you offer.

In this example, you are going to hear a story about a real scrapper named Nathan. He worked hard from sunup to sundown to get as many new customers as he possibly could. Over the years, he established himself as the "guy to talk to" about getting rid of scrap metal.

What most people didn't know about Nathan was that he was an avid reader. He understood that leaders were always readers. He would dedicate 30-45 minutes of his day every morning to reading about his industry's latest developments, as well as many entrepreneurial stories.

While driving in his car on his way to a job, in

between jobs, and even on his way home, he would listen to audiobooks on his smartphone. He would educate himself on different entrepreneurial endeavors while he was driving. He would also listen to audiobooks on his headphones while he worked. He would put his headphones on and listen to take his mind off the hard work he had to do. He figured he was getting an education and a workout, while being paid at the same time.

Nathan realized that while other people got their education and were rewarded with A's, B's, C's, D's, and F's, he was getting his education on the job while being rewarded with Franklin's, Grant's, Jackson's, Hamilton's, Lincoln's, and Washington's. He figured that while everybody else was paying $10,000-$25,000 per year and more to get rewarded with A's, B's, C's, D's, and F's, and a piece of paper at the end of all their homework and testing, he was out hustling the streets, making, saving, and reinvesting into his business more than double that amount year after year. He knew he was building a business for himself that would serve him well for many years in his future.

On his way to a job one Saturday morning, Nathan was listening to an audiobook just like he always did. This day was different though. He heard something in this audiobook that inspired a thought. It inspired him to think about changing his approach to how he offered his services. In the audiobook he learned about the moving company, PODS, founded in 1998. He also learned about the moving company, Two Men And A Truck, founded in 1985.

In the audiobook he learned the difference between the two moving companies and how they operated differently from one another, yet both were still national franchises. Both managed to scale nationally in the same space, yet both took very different approaches.

He realized that Two Men And A Truck was a full-service moving company whose mode of operation was to literally send two men and a truck, usually in a large box van moving truck, out to their customer's homes. Once the two men and a truck arrived at the customer's home, they would enter the home, pack up everything, load it into the box truck for the customer, then drive it to the new destination, take it in the house, and place it in the rooms for their customer. They had a few different packages that they offered their customers like any other business, but this was their basic modus operandi. Nathan realized this company took a traditional hands-on approach to moving its customers.

The second thing he noticed in this audiobook was the functionality of a moving company by the name of PODS. He realized that PODS took more of a hands-off approach to moving people from one place to another. The way PODS operated their organization really resonated with Nathan because it seemed so much more efficient and streamlined. He realized the way PODS set themselves apart from traditional moving companies was they offered portable containers they would drop off at a customer's home so the customer could take their time loading it themselves for an agreed upon amount of days. Once the customer was finished loading the container, a PODS delivery driver would come out, pick up the container, and either drive it to their storage facility to be stored or take it straight to the customer's desired destination. They even offered storage services for their customers in the event their customer had to be out of their old place before their new place was fully ready to move into. He also realized PODS had multiple packages they offered their customers. These were a few key points of service that set PODS apart from traditional moving companies.

Nathan learned that PODS had the type of customer who was capable of doing their own lifting and loading, or just simply wanted to for one reason or another. Whereas Two Men And A Truck tended to attract the customer who wasn't capable of doing their own loading and moving, or simply didn't want to do it themselves.

[113]

It was in this moment that Nathan had an epiphany that would change the way he operated his business forever. He realized he had been taking a traditional approach to the way he was offering his services to his customers.

Now, Nathan didn't mind doing the work, and at times he even enjoyed the workout. He had just come to realize he could make his business much more efficient if he changed a couple things he had been saying on the phone before he went out to a customer's home to remove their items. The approach that PODS took really resonated because he realized if he could do something similar to that in his own business, then not only would it save him time onsite, but it would also free up more time for him to focus on things like marketing and advertising his services.

If he could spend more time on advertising and marketing his services, then he knew it would result in more calls, which would result in more jobs, which would result in him having a larger business and ultimately more cash in his pocket. At this point, he was halfway to his job so he turned off his audiobook, pulled his truck over, grabbed a pen and a notepad, and started to write down his strategy. He thought: *How can I operate more like the PODS moving company?*

After pondering for 10 minutes or so, much to his

surprise, an idea came to him.

After sitting in silence for a few minutes and doing some critical thinking, he decided to make some changes to the questions he'd been asking his customers prior to showing up at their home. Over the next four months, Nathan consistently implemented the following strategy to every one of his phone calls, as well as recorded his results with each customer using a pen and a notepad.

What he decided to do was ask his customers the following simple questions leading up to setting the appointment. After receiving his customer's phone call and listening to his customer's needs, he would say to his customer, "I understand you want to get rid of some unwanted material, and I am definitely the man for the job. Now let me ask you, where is everything situated on your property? By that I mean is everything going to be in the backyard? On the side of the house? In the garage? Upstairs? Downstairs?"

He would then pause and wait for the customer to reply with their answer.

Sometimes things would be all ready to go, sitting out on the driveway ready for pickup. This was his favorite kind of stop to make and he'd always wished he could get more of them because they were always quick and easy. His new strategy was to realize exactly that, more of the quick and easy jobs!

However, most of the time his customers were calling with a variety of metals situated in various places, such as the customer's backyard, some were in the garage, and some were in the shed out back, etc. When he would take a call from this type of customer with this type of need, he would implement his strategy at this exact point in the conversation. He would ask his customer the "holy grail" of questions: "If I…could you…?"

This was one of the smartest things he had ever implemented in his business. He would say to his customer, "I can understand why you want to get this taken care of. Nobody wants to have things laying around their house and I want to see you get it done ASAP as well. Now, *if I* can get you onto the schedule as soon as tomorrow [or whatever day the customer had suggested they would like to have service done], then *could you* possibly have everything gathered in one spot, as close as possible to where I'm going to park and load it up for you?" He would say, "I'm not trying to be lazy about the work or anything like that, but I can get this out of your hair for sure if it's all ready to go and I don't have to spend as much time onsite, which would allow me to get to the rest of my appointments on time as well."

At that point he would stop talking and wait for the customer's response. In general, about 70% of the time, what he would hear was, "Sure! No problem! I'll have it ready to go." Often, the customer would have their children or grandchildren take care of it for them. Sometimes a neighbor or a brother-in-law.

Roughly 20% of the time, he would hear answers like, "Yes, I can get most of it, but I don't have a dolly so I can't move the refrigerator or the appliances."

This was still a tremendous help for him and it reduced his workload considerably by not having to walk back and forth across his customer's property multiple times carrying weight.

Approximately 10% of the time he would just hear the customer say "no" they couldn't, for one reason or another. Most of the time when he was told no, and the customer wasn't willing to help out, it had been for various reasons such as they were elderly, they didn't have the strength, they didn't have a dolly, they were too busy, they were disabled, etc.

Overall, the majority of the time he would get his desired response, receiving help from his customers with performing a good portion of the labor by having them gather it themselves. This way he would only have to show up, quickly load, and move on.

Nathan implemented this strategy every single time he took a call from a customer. Almost immediately he realized that his workload had gone down a considerable amount. He wasn't nearly as physically exhausted when he got home from jobs. He was also getting home much earlier in the day with just as much money, after putting out much less physical effort. This, in turn, gave him the time and energy necessary to focus on his marketing and advertising with Craigslist, flyers, door hangers, and business cards.

This subtle change in his day-to-day operation is what eventually separated Nathan from the pack. This is what would set him apart from all of his competitors who were doing things the conventional way. Prior to listening to the audiobook on that Saturday morning, Nathan had also been doing things the conventional way, which limited him to the amount of jobs he was able to complete per day. By recruiting help from his customers prior to showing up, he set himself apart from his competitors in the same fashion that PODS set themselves apart from Two Men And A Truck, as well as many other traditional moving companies.

He was now able to handle a larger volume of stops due to becoming more efficient with his loading process. What he noticed was that the customer's participation in helping him with the loading process actually formed a different type of relationship between him and the customer because it was something they did together, in order to help each other out.

Remember, one paragraph in an audiobook on entrepreneurship that Nathan listened to on his way to work changed the course of his business and his life permanently. Not only that, but the audiobook he had listened to was written about a completely unrelated industry from the one he was operating in. Nathan was smart enough to know that the principles he was reading about could be carried over to his own industry and be applied effectively to help him with his own business.

In conclusion, if you take nothing else from this example, Nathan would hope that you would implement his notorious question into your phone calls with your customers: "If I…could you…?" Also, Nathan would recommend you continue reading books and listening to audiobooks as often as possible. One single paragraph changed his life for the better.

This concludes the story of Nathan and how he separated himself from his competition by becoming more efficient.

Lesson 20

How to Get Above Average Prices on Appliances and Build Relationships with Businesses

First, you'll want to get online and find a list of local appliance stores, as well as local appliance repair services. Either call or walk in with a flyer and a business card. Leave your information with the store manager or the owner, if possible. You can leave your information with the secretary but nine times out of 10 they've been instructed to not let any salespeople get past them. You are not a salesperson per se, but you want some of the owner's attention and their job is to be the gatekeeper. They don't know the difference. Just get the owner. The manager is second-best. At least get the owner's name and find them on Facebook, or some other way, and make sure you get your information to them effectively.

For your new and used appliance dealers, you'll want to ask them if they haul away unwanted appliances free of charge for people who haven't purchased new appliances from them first. Appliance store owners get calls from customers asking about disposal all the time. When they tell you no, they don't offer the service unless somebody has made a purchase, you tell them that is exactly what you do and that you would love to leave some cards behind so they can direct their customers to an honest and ethical appliance removal service that will not charge them.

At this point, you will want to ask if they would be interested in buying some of your more quality appliances that you get from your customers when you do residential pickups (the ones that may be a little bit newer or just a more reputable brand). Ask for a good cell phone number or email address so you can send pictures or video to them when you come across some decent units. If you're talking to the manager, he might actually have the authority to make this decision. If not, you really want to communicate to the manager that this is your intent. Do whatever you can to help him pass this along to the owner or whoever can make these kinds of decisions.

It's fair for you to get 3 to 4 times what scrap value is because the owner is going to make 5 to 10 times what he pays you, if not more. Everybody wins! This is why I would recommend you ask him what he would be willing to pay first. Let him throw out a number. Make sure you understand what current prices are in the scrap market so you know if he is offering you a fair price. One good online resource for this is scrapmonster.com. This isn't always going to be perfectly accurate compared to your local market when you call around, but it's a good resource to check for major and sudden market changes.

A lot of times you will find that you will get the higher price on popular models. Earning 3 to 4 times what you would get at the scrapyard is worth the extra effort as long as you don't have to go too far out of your way to make it happen. Preferably you would have somewhere to store these items, like a garage or a storage unit. If not, just make sure you're not traveling too far out of your way.

You have resources to check the market. I suggest you stay on top of that before making a deal with anybody, so you can get a fair price every time. This will take you 30 seconds online, so don't be lazy. Remember, in this lesson we are not necessarily talking about going to a scrapyard; these are additional options for you to turn larger profits when the opportunity strikes.

You should repeat this process with multiple store owners. You need to do whatever is necessary to get your phone number into the hands of the store owner or manager. If you can win the secretary over, that's a bonus too. She may remember you and refer business to you as well. Your goal is to repeat this process with every single new or used appliance business listed in your area. The more of these contacts you open up, the more opportunity you create for yourself.

Now, what have you done here? You have effectively created a potential stream of referral income with multiple appliance repairmen, as well as appliance store owners. Keep in mind, most appliance stores recycle their own scrap themselves. Some will have a roll off dumpster on their property and they just call to have it picked up. Remember, scrap metal and old appliances are not the primary reasons you are there, they are secondary. You will get plenty of appliances from your residential customers and also from some of the store owners who don't offer haul away services. Most already know how to recycle and they're probably getting a pretty good price.

Your primary reason for reaching out to them is to provide them with an extended service for their business that you are offering to their customers about how to solve the problem of getting rid of their old appliances. Often, if they do sell new appliances, then they will offer a free haul away service. However, some of them do not, which is why it is good for you to speak to all appliance stores, whether they're doing repairs, selling used appliances, or strictly selling new appliances. The point is they all deal in appliances. If you want to catch a fish, then you gotta go where the fish are.

Making moves like this puts you in a position to have the store owner or repair business acting as your salesman, while making their business look good as well. If the owner is strictly dealing in used appliances, then they may also even be willing to buy the appliances from you after they've referred you to their customers because they don't have the time to take care of it themselves.

Trust me, these types of things can grow over time, if you're persistent. Whether you're hustling or in business for yourself, it's about building relationships. What better way than to start out offering a service for free. At the same time, you can turn a profit while offering a convenience to the appliance repair man/store owner and his customers. You see, he benefits because he can extend a service to his customers that he doesn't currently offer himself. Or if he does, he may think of you when he's too busy to handle it himself. This makes him look good because he solves a problem for his customers. The customer is now happy with the appliance repair man/store owner because he solved their problem.

You've also formed a relationship with the appliance

repair man/store owner. This is because now, every time you get a popular appliance of any kind in your own travels, he's agreed to let you send him pictures or videos of such appliances. This makes it really convenient for you to see if he's willing to purchase them from you for more than what you could've earned at the scrapyard. In this case, you've made more than you would've ever made at the scrapyard. Also, worst case, if none of the appliance store owners/repairmen want to purchase your appliance at a higher price, then at least you still have an appliance to scrap with potentially extractable material inside of it, depending on the appliance. I'd recommend trying something like this right after you've read about it. This should be eye opening. I hope you understand the longer you stay in this game, the more deals you get will continue to increase in number and in size.

This is a great way to get some practice with no money on the line out of your own pocket. This is one strategy that your average scrapper, who is just going around and taking metal off the street on garbage day when everybody has their trash cans out, is probably not doing. By the way, you can do the whole garbage day thing yourself and you'll probably make money. I have never done that and I don't intend to. I want to elevate your thinking just a little bit above the average person in this industry, so that you start out at a higher level, with higher goals, and ultimately higher income.

We will be moving on from appliances at this point. The plan is to explain how to obtain above average amounts of all different types of scrap metal by implementing a strategy. We're going to move on now to your iron strategy.

Lesson 21

How to Get Commercial Accounts for Scrap Iron

This strategy is very important because you will usually make more money with iron than you will with appliances or tin metals. It is one of the more common metals that you will collect. In general, prepared iron is anything iron that is measured at less than 4 feet in length, less than 18 inches in width, and greater than ¼ inch thick.

Iron material that is larger than prepared iron is considered unprepared iron. Iron also has a category known as "shearable" iron. The price for this is usually in between prepared iron and unprepared iron. Most places just buy from the general public as either prepared iron or unprepared iron.

For the purpose of this book we are just going to use two categories. Earlier in the book you learned about what types of iron are considered prepared iron. Here is where you will learn how to find them in the same fashion as you learned to find appliances.

This will be slightly different and will require that you talk to some people once again. This will be another way to make deals with multiple business owners, without taking any money out of your pocket. However, sometimes you may decide it's worth your time to make a purchase and lay some money down in order to secure a deal. For starters we are going to focus strictly on the lower risk strategy so you don't get hurt financially in the beginning. You can learn to take calculated risks later. Right now we're trying to maximize your income.

Okay, now that you understand the measurements for prepared iron, what do you look for? Who do you talk to? What follows is an example of where to go and what offer to make when you get there.

Start by doing a Google search. You're going to seek out and create a list of prospect businesses, including but not limited to auto repair shops, metal working companies, CNC machine shops, welders, etc. There are many others, but for now I would start here because you will have a better chance with these businesses.

Earlier you were given examples of what constitutes prepared iron. Your strategy will be similar to the example with the appliance store. GET THE OWNER or manager and try to bypass the secretary as best you can. If the secretary is the only one available, at least try to give her your business card or your flyer, and make sure she has your contact info. Ask when the owner or manager will be available and do everything in your power to get their attention. You might want to bring in coffee and donuts one day. A $5-$10 box of doughnuts could get you in the door and bring you repeat business for years! It's the little things that help you stand out among your competitors.

Iron is going to be much more profitable than appliances because you're going to have more weight and it's going to be sold at a higher value. In this lesson you'll learn fundamental skills to help you make a professional sounding offer, as well as some basic negotiation techniques.

Negotiating, if you're like most people, may scare the hell out of you. It takes a lot of nerve and it takes a lot of guts. This is different, so just keep reading and trust the process.

It's important to remember that you're dealing with a business owner now. Some are savvy and some are not. Either way, they are no better than you. So conduct yourself with integrity and confidence, even if you have to fake it at first.

In this example we're going to use a mechanic shop for our scenario. The mechanic—we'll call him Johnny—also understands that iron has value to some degree. It's likely you're not the first person who has come to him looking for metal. Don't let that bother you. Nobody he's ever dealt with is any better than you either. The only difference is they had the courage to walk through his door first.

Most guys like Johnny will have a dedicated area for scrap parts. It's usually going to be somewhere in the corner of the shop or toward the back near where they work on the cars. This is like a trash bin for Johnny. After he replaces an old part, it has to go somewhere.

If possible, try to locate his scrap pile so you can point it out while you're making an offer. This way there's no chance for the mechanic to tell you he's got nothing for you and to beat it.

Here's how you approach the situation, assuming you're able to get directly to the mechanic who is in charge. You're going to tell him that you are a scrapper. You've been doing this for a really long time and you're looking to build a lasting relationship with several mechanics in the area. Don't be gimmicky and try not to sound scripted if you've practiced what you're going to say.

Once you've told him your intentions, get straight to the point and ask for his business. Tell him you can be trusted and you are reliable. Let him know you would like to put him on a biweekly or monthly pickup schedule. This of course depends upon how fast he accumulates his scrap. In this case you'll pick a set date when you're going to stop by and get rid of all his unwanted scrap material. Some will be iron and some will be tin, but here you'll be dealing with primarily prepared iron which is the "good stuff" when we're talking about ferrous metal.

Okay, at this point Johnny knows why you're there and he knows your intentions. You haven't wasted his time and you've gotten straight to the point. He may tell you somebody else already provides this service for him. He may also tell you he takes it in to recycle himself and he doesn't need your services.

This may be true, but here's your response to that. Let him know you plan on being in this industry for a very long time. Your response should sound something like this: "Johnny, hey look man, I heard you when you said you have another guy taking care of this. Now, I don't want to step on anybody's toes, but I feel I would be doing you a disservice by not at least letting you know I am also here for you in case the other guy ends up bailing on you. Not only that, but I can provide better service while being on time." Here's the kicker, let him know you can give him an equal or better percentage of the profit.

You want Johnny to understand that because you take so much steel to the scrapyard, they treat you as a high-volume commercial customer. This isn't the type of language coming out of your average scrapper's mouth. You're standing there, dressed nice, with a professional business card and flyer in your hand. You've been very polite to the secretary and you've been very polite to Johnny. You're using words like "high-volume" and "commercial" in the same sentence. Most scrappers will show up high, can't spell volume, and don't know what commercial means! If you feel you've made a connection with Johnny, you may want to crack a joke like this just to leave him an impression.

At this point, you have planted a seed with Johnny and his wheels may be turning a little bit. This is a good thing; this is what you want. He may be thinking: *Percentage? What do you mean percentage? My scrap guy is taking this for free. I really don't have much here every month, but what am I missing?*

Note: I don't know what month and year you decided to pick this book up, but if you're reading this when the market is considered low, believe it or not, that's the time you want to establish all your accounts. You may not get as much for your pound as "they used to pay." You will hear this a lot from low level scrappers. Just don't be discouraged by this. Their chatter has nothing to do with your "long game" plan and your endgame results.

Scrap is a volatile market, but there is still profit in it. Ask yourself this question: what happens when you secure multiple accounts while the price of scrap is low? You establish relationships with Johnny and other mechanics like him, and you are in control of the flow of this reoccurring scrap metal when the price of iron starts to increase in value. It could take a sudden jump in your favor and stay that way for years! You will have positioned yourself on the ground floor of a boom in the scrap metal industry before it happens. This is right where you want to be!

Now back to you and Johnny. Johnny probably has a general idea of the price of scrap, or he may not. If he has a small amount, he'll probably think: *How can this guy afford to give me anything for the amount that I have?* Just let Johnny know you still believe he deserves something in return for the opportunity to do business with him, even if it's just a little something.

At this point, he may ask what you're offering. I would recommend in a down market, that you offer him 30% of the profit, if, and only if, your competition is already getting it for free. You want to start with 30% because if the market increases, then he may ask you for a larger percentage once the word gets out and you can bump him up over time to a 50/50 split. Anything less than 30% is a little tacky for an offer. I would just wait for him to ask for it. Remember, you are providing a free service and it is worth your fair share.

Note: Your initial objective is to offer your free service in exchange for the metal. Don't mention anything about a percentage until you learn that it will be necessary to potentially secure the account. If the other guy is giving him a percentage, simply tell him you will match it. If you have to, just beat it by 5%.

You're going to tell Johnny you can bring 30% of the profit back to him when you finish all your stops, either the same day or the following day. If he's already getting nothing from your competition, then he's got nothing to lose by placing his trust in the fact that you will be back with some cash for him. Remember, right now you are just focusing on securing his account. This is a simple and small deal. Your goal is to secure a number of these deals to form one solid income stream. With this strategy you will be carving out a percentage of profit for yourself, with no out of pocket cost to you.

Note: You always want to "assume the sale" through your language and your body language. That's why you'll offer to bring Johnny's percentage back to him that same day, or the following day at the latest. It implies you are ready to handle this immediately and that you're expecting to. Plus, now there's something to gain for Johnny.

To digress momentarily, you will not get every deal. A lot of times when you're told no, it actually means not right now. So even after you've talked to Johnny and let's say he tells you no, you'll still want to come back and check with him every couple of weeks so that he can see you're serious and that you can keep a schedule.

I recommend checking with Johnny every Friday or every other Friday. Why? Because Johnny is probably going to be in a good mood on Fridays. Most mechanics are looking forward to the weekend. Johnny might also need some beer money and may not have time to run to the scrapyard. That's where you come in. Who do you think he's going to think of from now on after you've made it that much easier for him to pick up a 12-pack on the way to that barbecue he's been planning on all week? Take good care of your customers; it pays dividends in the end!

Back to Johnny. If he tells you he does it himself, that's okay too. Just make the same offer and let him know if he ever runs into a situation where he can't deal with it because he is too busy working under those hoods, that you are here and you will be here for the long haul. You'll want to stop by and ask him every week or two for his business again. If you do this right and you are polite, he may get sick of you, but in my experience guys like Johnny eventually end up folding because either they are sick of telling you no, or they just plain feel sorry for you. When he does finally give in, wait to do your money dance until *after* you've at least gotten around the corner! Try not to look surprised either; you don't want to give him the sense he just made a deal with a rookie.

Note: You will also experience various types of non-ferrous metals when you're dealing with guys like Johnny. They will come in the form of starters, alternators, air-conditioning units, radiators, auto wiring, etc. This will increase the amount of money you make while dealing with Johnny. I recommend you make your offer to Johnny straight across the board. It's 30% on all metals, both ferrous and non-ferrous. You will be receiving 70% as your portion of the profit from his iron, as well as his more valuable nonferrous metals.

At the end of the day, if you do have to go 50/50 from the beginning to secure the deal, I would still recommend you do it. If he's got a lot of weight and he indicates he has higher volume, then you may consider settling for 40% to you and 60% to Johnny, or even more if he has several tons. You just want to start negotiating from 30% so you have some room to negotiate up if necessary.

In a down market, most of the time you won't need to negotiate much. It's when the market gets good that the sharks come out and cause things to become very competitive. This is why you want to make sure you take very good care of your customer when you acquire their account. Once you've secured and gotten control of this account, the scrap metal market could increase a month or two down the road. If this happens, then your 70% portion of the deal automatically increases as well, with no additional effort on your part.

If you take good care of your customers and make yourself hard to replace by being punctual, honest, and reliable, then you will likely retain this account month after month, year after year. You can take this strategy with you into the multiple businesses listed earlier and use the exact same approach no matter what type of material they have. At the end of the day, it all comes down to that percentage.

Epilogue

In this three-part book you have learned from A to Z everything you need to know to get started making cash today with scrap metal recycling. In Part 1 you received an introduction to scrap metal recycling, and most likely recovered a portion of the money you invested, if not all of it, and potentially turned a profit as well. You learned how to identify the different types of metals, as well as how to locate a scrapyard and what to do when you get there. If you've had no previous experience with scrap metal recycling, I am confident that a new world has been revealed to you. A world in which moneymaking possibilities weren't present prior to reading Part 1 of the book. If this is true for you, then this book has served its purpose well.

In Part 2 and 3 you learned some advanced online and offline marketing strategies through character stories on how to acquire larger quantities of scrap metal. This in turn could potentially lead to larger quantities of cash in your pocket, if you apply the knowledge given and take action. Each character illustrated in this book had their own strategy and way of doing business. It is my hope that from their examples you will learn to do the same for yourself.

This book could go on for hours and even days giving you all the details and layers there are to understanding all there is to know about scrap metal recycling. However, as promised in the beginning of this book, it has been condensed down to an easy to digest and understand format.

At this point, you have learned all you need to know to get started and advance quickly. If you apply the knowledge illustrated in this book, based on the examples you have read, you will be starting out at a much higher level than anybody who is just discovering the industry. Not only that, but you've probably already earned your money back for the education after doing a test run.

I truly hope this book has served you and opened your eyes to a new world of possibilities. May the scrap gods bless you and your bank account for years to come. Now go make some money!

P.S. If you've gotten value from reading this book, please leave me a review on Amazon. Every review is important and helps readers discover my books and improve their lives as well. Thank you in advance!

For more about future projects and events please visit www.milesbroderson.com.

About the Author

Miles H. Broderson AKA "Hank Broderson" was born and raised in Oroville, California, a small town located an hour north of the state capitol, Sacramento. He spent much of his youth on and around Lake Oroville with friends and family. There he would enjoy various activities ranging from fishing, camping, boating, riding bikes, etc.

At the age of 17 he became interested in entrepreneurship. While still working his first job as a garage door installer, he began delivering firewood on weekends. This followed his grandfather's passing as his grandfather was in the firewood business. He had been helping his grandmother sell the rest of his grandfather's stockpile that year, while earning some extra money in the process. Little did he know at the time, this would turn out to be his first taste of entrepreneurship, which would make any other pathway he attempted unsustainable.

As the years went by, he found himself bouncing between a handful of jobs, trying to find his way in life. By the age of 21 he owned a vending machine business. By the age of 25 he was a partner in a scrap metal recycling facility.

He currently resides in Southern California and is the owner of a successful junk removal company offering scrap metal removal services and more. His company has evolved from scrap metal removal to junk removal and then even further into machine work. He provides a variety of equipment services such as bobcat/skid steer, as well as tractor services, delivery services, and more.

With the understanding that the scrap metal industry may not be for everybody long-term, he maintains his philosophy that it is a strong catalyst to break into other industries and evolve into whatever one chooses. That is his entire reason for publishing this book. His intent is to shed light on an industry that may open up new opportunities and potentially change the course of your life forever!